In the Ring

Main Features

Page 2
Discover boxing's violent past

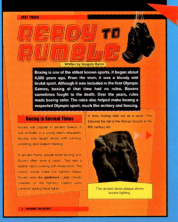

Page 18
All about boxing today

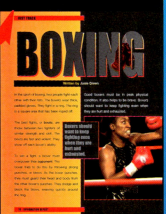

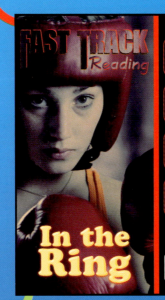

Page 10
Johnny has a tough decision to make

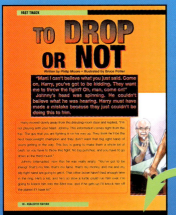

Page 24
Will Jackson get his dream job?

Other Features

Rules 8	List 30
Terms 16	Glossary 31
Diagram 17	Index 32
Chart 23	

FAST TRACK

READY TO RUMBLE

Written by Gregory Byron

> Boxing is one of the oldest known sports. It began about 4,000 years ago. From the start, it was a bloody and brutal sport. Although it was included in the first Olympic Games, boxing at that time had no rules. Boxers sometimes fought to the death. Over the years, rules made boxing safer. The rules also helped make boxing a respected Olympic sport, much like archery and fencing.

Boxing in Ancient Times

Boxing was popular in ancient Greece. It was included in a young man's education. Boxing was taught along with running, wrestling, and weapon training.

In ancient Rome, people loved boxing, too. Boxers often wore a *cestus*. This was a leather hand covering with metal studs. The cestus would make the fighters bleed. Boxers were like **gladiators**. Large crowds cheered on the fighters. Deaths were common during these fights.

In time, boxing died out as a sport. This followed the fall of the Roman Empire in the fifth century AD.

This ancient stone plaque shows boxers fighting.

Boxing in the 1600s

Boxing reappeared in England in the late 1600s. It remained a cruel sport. Bouts were usually fought without rules. There were no gloves – fighters used their bare knuckles. Bare-fisted fights could last up to seven hours. Bouts did not end until there was a knockout, or until one fighter could not continue. Fighters were sometimes killed.

Although boxing was illegal, it was popular. People saw the fights as entertainment.

Boxing in the 1700s

In 1719, James Figg became the first British boxing champion.

Later in the century, an English bare-knuckle **prizefighter** named Jack Broughton tried to turn boxing into an acceptable sport. In 1743, Broughton introduced the first set of rules for boxing. The rules stated that the fighters must fight inside a square area that was chalked on the ground. Only the referee and boxers were allowed in this area.

Other rules were –

- A boxer has 30 seconds to get up if knocked down
- No hitting or wrestling below the belt
- No hitting when the opponent is down
- The round is over with a knockdown

These rules helped the sport of boxing. But bare-knuckle fighting was still allowed. So were kicking, wrestling, and gouging. There was also no set number of rounds. Fights lasted until one of the fighters was very badly beaten and could not go on.

Jack Broughton also wanted people to use boxing gloves. The gloves he used were known as mufflers.

An engraving of a boxing match in 1788

FAST TRACK

Boxing in the 1800s

Prizefighting was very popular in London during the mid 1800s. But someone needed to take control of the sport. A boxing official named John Graham Chambers took this role. In the 1860s, Chambers wrote the Marquess of Queensberry boxing rules. These rules helped change the image of boxing as a brutal sport.

The Queensberry Rules stated that boxing gloves must be used for all fights. They said that bouts must last a limited number of rounds. Gouging and wrestling were not allowed, and there had to be a count of ten seconds before a floored boxer was disqualified. These rules are still used today.

At first, the Queensberry Rules were not widely accepted. Bare-knuckle contests were still fought. The last bare-knuckle heavyweight champion was an American. His name was John L. Sullivan, but he was known as the "Boston Strong Boy." He fought and won the last bare-knuckle fight in 1889. This was against Jake Kilrain. The fight went for 75 rounds. This famous fight marked the beginning of the popularity of boxing in America

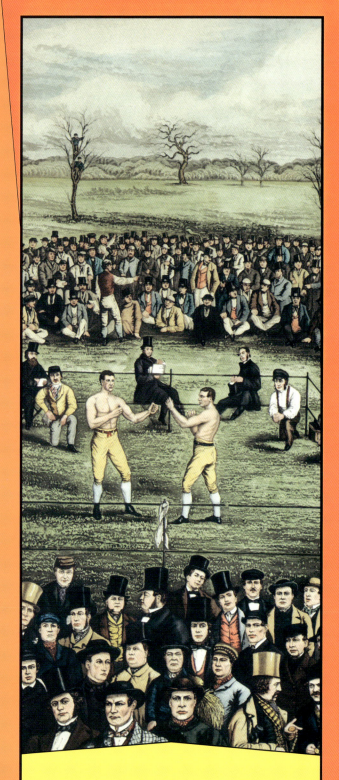

Crowds watch an open-air boxing match in the 1800s.

4 - INFORMATION REPORT

Modern Boxing

The Queensberry Rules became the basis for modern boxing rules. They helped boxing become the respected athletic sport it is today. There have been many great boxers in the twentieth century.

Muhammad Ali (US)

Cassius Clay was this boxer's original name. During his career, he changed his name to Muhammad Ali. He first came onto the boxing scene in 1960. At that time, he won the light heavyweight Olympic gold medal in Rome. He was only 18 years old. Four years later, he went on to win the world heavyweight championship. He said that in the ring he aimed to "float like a butterfly, but sting like a bee."

"Sugar" Ray Leonard (US)

"Sugar" Ray Leonard won a gold medal in boxing at the 1976 Olympics. During the bout, he had a picture of his wife and son taped to his sock. Three years later, he won the World Boxing Council welterweight **title**. Then he fought Roberto Duran twice in 1980. In the first fight, he lost his title. In the second, he regained his title from Duran.

In 1981, Leonard defeated Thomas Hearns for the world welterweight title. Hearns had been unbeaten up to that time. In 1987, Leonard defeated Marvin Hagler for the middleweight championship title.

Muhammad Ali (left) and "Sugar" Ray Leonard

FAST TRACK

Jeff Fenech (Australia)

In 1985, Jeff Fenech came into the **limelight**. He took the world champion bantamweight title after only seven bouts. Over the next four years, he remained unbeaten. He took world titles at three different weights – bantamweight, light featherweight, and featherweight.

Mike Tyson (US)

In 1986, Mike Tyson became the youngest heavyweight world champion in history. He was 20 years old. Mike Tyson was a very aggressive fighter. In 1997, when he was fighting Evander Holyfield, Tyson lost control of his temper. He bit a chunk out of Holyfield's right ear. Tyson was disqualified for this act, and fined. He was also banned from boxing for two years.

Jeff Fenech is now in the US Boxing Hall of Fame.

Mike Tyson during a fight against Brian Nielsen in 2001

Evander Holyfield (US)

In 1990, Evander Holyfield beat James "Buster" Douglas. This won him the heavyweight title. Holyfield went on to win the heavyweight championship two more times. He did this by defeating Riddick Bowe in 1993 and Mike Tyson in 1996.

Evander Holyfield holds a Men of the Year Award, which he was awarded in 1998.

Lennox Lewis (UK)

Lennox Lewis turned professional after winning the 1988 Olympic heavyweight gold medal. In March 1999, he and Evander Holyfield fought each other in New York. The judges' decision was that the fight was a draw. Eight months later, the two fighters faced each other again, and Lewis won strongly. The century closed with the British-born boxer as one of the world's heavyweight champions. In 2002, he was still a world champion.

Lennox Lewis salutes a crowd.

Boxing is as popular today as it ever was. All around the world today, people box and watch boxing, just as they have over the centuries.

FAST TRACK

Marquess of Queensberry Rules

Rule 1: To be a fair stand-up boxing match in a 24-feet (7.3-m) ring, or as near that size as practicable.

Rule 2: No wrestling or hugging allowed.

Rule 3: The rounds to be of three minutes' duration, and one minute's time between rounds.

Rule 4: If either man falls through weakness or otherwise, he must get up unassisted, ten seconds to be allowed him to do so, the other man meanwhile to return to his corner, and when the fallen man is on his legs the round is to be resumed and continued until the three minutes have expired. If one man fails to come to the scratch in the ten seconds allowed, it shall be in the power of the referee to give his award in favor of the other man.

Rule 5: A man hanging on the ropes in a helpless state, with his toes off the ground, shall be considered down.

Rule 6: No seconds or any other person to be allowed in the ring during the rounds.

 Rule 7: Should the contest be stopped by any unavoidable interference, the referee to name the time and place as soon as possible for finishing the contest; so that the match must be won and lost, unless the backers of both men agree to draw the stakes.

 Rule 8: The gloves to be fair-sized boxing gloves of the best quality and new.

 Rule 9: Should a glove burst or come off, it must be replaced to the referee's satisfaction.

 Rule 10: A man on one knee is considered down and if struck is entitled to the stakes.

 Rule 11: No shoes or boots with springs allowed.

 Rule 12: The contest in all other respects to be governed by revised rules of the London Prize Ring.

FAST TRACK

TO DROP OR NOT

Written by Philip Moore • Illustrated by Bruce Potter

"Man! I can't believe what you just said. Come on, Harry, you've got to be kidding. They want me to throw the fight? Oh, man, come on!"

Johnny's head was spinning. He couldn't believe what he was hearing. Harry must have made a mistake because they just couldn't be doing this to him.

Harry moved slowly away from the dressing-room door and replied, "I'm not playing with your head, Johnny. This information comes right from the top. The guy that you are fighting is on his way up. They think he'll be the next heavyweight champion and they don't want that big right hand of yours getting in the way. This boy is going to make them a whole lot of cash, so you have to throw this fight. No big punches, and you have to go down in the third round."

Johnny interrupted, now that he was really angry, "You've got to be joking! That's my title, that's my fame, that's my money, and me and my big right hand are going to get it. That other boxer hasn't had enough time in the ring. He's a kid, and he's so slow a turtle could run him over. I'm going to knock him into the 83rd row, and if he gets up I'll knock him off the planet if I have to!"

10 - REALISTIC FICTION

Johnny knew he was ranting, but he couldn't believe what he had just heard. He was trying to fight what Harry had said with words, but most of all he was trying to convince himself that years of hard work hadn't come to this. No way was he going to give up his dream of becoming the Heavyweight Champion of the World.

Harry grabbed Johnny's shoulder.

"Please, sit down, Johnny, and listen carefully to what I have to say," he urged.

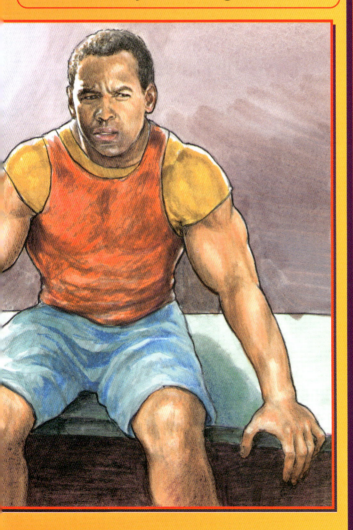

Johnny sank down onto the massage table but still towered over the aging man.

Harry continued, "I want you to listen and listen good, Johnny. I've been a trainer for a long time. I've seen a lot of things happen in the boxing industry. These people who want you to throw the fight, they're powerful, and they've got a lot of influence. You know what I mean, Johnny?"

There was a flicker of sadness in Harry's steel-blue eyes as he continued, "You haven't been fighting well since Charlie died. Your heart just hasn't been in it. I know you lost more than a coach, but Johnny, you're not focused.

"This is what they are offering – you throw this fight, then they'll organize a couple of smaller fights for you that you will definitely win. You keep the money from those fights, then retire. That should be enough money to look after you and your family."

"And what if I don't?" Johnny said, standing up defiantly.

Harry looked at the floor as he answered, "These people have influence. You won't get another fight. You and your family, you'll all be out on the street. That whole lifestyle that you've been living will be out the window. That's the choice you have to make."

FAST TRACK

Harry turned and walked out of the room. He didn't even look back as he walked through the door.

Johnny could feel the anger rising within him, the same anger that took control when he was caught on the ropes, stranded with nowhere to go. The walls were closing in all around him. He grabbed his bag and ran for the back door of the gym. It led him out to the street.

The winter wind cut into Johnny's face, but even its icy blast wasn't enough to cool his raging anger. He needed distance between him and this place, so he kept running. He was headed for the only place that he really felt secure. He was headed for his family.

Maria could tell that there was something wrong as soon as she opened the door. Johnny's usual smile was gone.

"What is it, Johnny? What's wrong?" Maria asked with concern in her voice.

Johnny didn't say anything. He just strode into the kitchen. Anger was pulsating through his body. Maria followed, trying to grab his hand, but Johnny didn't want to be touched and he pulled away.

He needed a release from the tension that was building within him. As they entered the kitchen, it was all too much for Johnny. He swung around, lifted his arm, and threw his training bag across the room. The bag slid across the tiled floor, smashing into a chair in the corner.

"That's it, Johnny," Maria's voice had a don't-argue-with-me tone to it. "You either calm down and tell me what has happened, or you go back to the gym. You know the rules, you leave your anger at the front door. This is our family home. What if one of the children saw their father acting like this?"

Johnny was startled by Maria's reaction, but he shouldn't have been surprised. It had been her love and strength that had pulled him off the streets when they had first met. She gave him the discipline he had never had when he was growing up. It was one of the things that he loved about her. It was from her that he learned that he could discipline himself to become a great boxer.

Johnny took a step back. He took a deep breath in. Then the whole story spilled out.

REALISTIC FICTION - 13

FAST TRACK

"Harry said they want me to throw the fight. He said they would give me a few easy fights, then I would have to retire. If I don't do what they say, it will all be over. They will make sure that I don't get another fight. Maria, they are trying to take my dream away, my chance to be the heavyweight champion. They think that I'm past my prime. They think I'm washed up."

Johnny hardly took a breath as he spoke, and all his sentences seemed to run together. He continued, "Boxing is the only thing I'm good at. It is all I know. Maria, how am I going to provide for my family? How am I going to look after you all?"

The huge muscles in Johnny's shoulders gave way first, shaking uncontrollably. Johnny was crumbling from the inside out. He collapsed onto the kitchen chair. The man who had knocked opponents all around the ring for ten years was crying. Maria went over to him and put her arms around him.

Quietly, she whispered reassuring words in his ear. "Don't worry, Johnny, everything is going to be OK. Together we can figure anything out. We've been through hard times before."

These comforting words helped Johnny regain his composure.

Johnny asked, "But what will I do? Throwing the fight goes against everything I believe in, but I have to or we won't have any money. I have to look after my family. I don't have a choice. I must do what they want."

Maria lovingly reached up and placed a hand on each of Johnny's cheeks, her fingers wiping his tears. Her words were comforting and supportive, "We knew you wouldn't be able to box forever, Johnny, but when you retire is your decision. No one else can tell you that. I've invested money from the day you won your first fight. Our family won't be wealthy, but we'll have more than enough, so don't you worry about that. You just have to decide when you have had enough and hang up your own gloves."

"You just keep on amazing me!" said Johnny as he pulled Maria closer to him. "I don't know what I'd do without you. You know what? Boxing isn't the same without Charlie. My heart isn't in it anymore. I'm going to give them one more fight. I'm going to beat this guy they think could be the heavyweight champion. That way I can always tell my children to be honest and give it all they've got. I'm not going to throw the fight. I'll leave this sport with my pride fully intact."

FAST TRACK

Boxing Terms

Here are some of the punches that are commonly used during a boxing bout —

feint – A faked punch. For example, a boxer may make a feint with their left hand, and then deliver an actual blow with their right hand.

jab – A quick blow in which the arm is extended straight from the shoulder. The jab is effective as both an offensive and a defensive weapon.

combination – Two or more fast punches in a row. A typical combination is a left, a right, then another left punch.

hook – A short blow to the side of the head or body.

straight – A long punch sent out straight from the shoulder with a lot of weight behind it.

swing – A swinging punch delivered from a long distance with all the boxer's body weight behind it.

uppercut – A very strong punch to the jaw. This is the most popular knockout blow.

Boxing Clothing and Equipment

1. Headguard
Boxers wear a padded headguard for protection. It covers the back and sides of the head and the ears. All boxers must wear a headguard when they spar. In a boxing bout, it is only the amateurs that must wear a headguard.

2. Mouth guard
This is a piece of hard rubber. It is worn in the mouth to protect the teeth.

3. Jersey
Amateurs and professional female boxers wear a jersey, but professional male boxers fight without a jersey.

4. Gloves
Boxers wear padded leather gloves to protect their hands. The gloves also protect the opponent from injury.

The weight of a pair of boxing gloves ranges from 6–12 ounces (170–340 g). Middleweight and lighter fighters usually wear 8-ounce (226.8-g) gloves, while heavier fighters use 10-ounce (283.5-g) gloves.

5. Bandages
Under the gloves, boxers' hands are tightly wrapped in soft bandages or tape for protection.

6. Protector
This is a hard plastic cup worn in the boxers' pants to protect the groin area from low punches.

7. Shorts
Boxers wear regulation shorts.

8. Boots
Boxers must wear boots with no heels.

DIAGRAM - 17

FAST TRACK

BOXING

Written by Josie Green

In the sport of boxing, two people fight each other with their fists. The boxers wear thick, padded gloves. They fight in a ring. The ring is a square area that has been roped off.

The best fights, or **bouts**, are those between two fighters of similar strength and skill. The bouts are fast and violent. They show off each boxer's ability.

To win a fight, a boxer must overpower their **opponent**. The boxer tries to do this by throwing strong punches, or blows. As the boxer punches, they must guard their head and body from the other boxer's punches. They dodge and block the blows, weaving quickly around the ring.

Good boxers must be in peak physical condition. It also helps to be brave. Boxers should want to keep fighting even when they are hurt and exhausted.

> Boxers should want to keep fighting even when they are hurt and exhausted.

18 - INFORMATION REPORT

The Ring

Boxing bouts take place inside a ring. The ring floor is covered in canvas. This canvas has rubber foam or felt mat underneath it to protect a fighter's head when they fall. The ring posts are also padded.

For amateur fights, the ring may measure from 16–20 square feet (4.9–6 sq m). For professional fights, the ring measurement is 16–24 square feet (4.9–7.3 sq m). The ring floor stands 3–4 feet (.9–1.2 m) higher than the main floor.

> Boxing rules were made to stop fighters from getting too seriously injured.

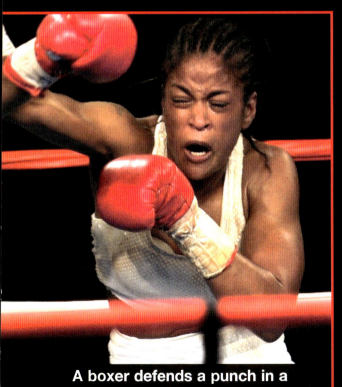

A boxer defends a punch in a professional bout.

Rounds

The time periods in a boxing bout are known as rounds. In an amateur bout, there are three rounds. Each round lasts two to three minutes. A professional bout is made up of ten or twelve rounds. Each round lasts three minutes. In all bouts, there is a one-minute rest between rounds.

The Rules

Boxing has always been considered a dangerous sport. Boxing rules were made to stop fighters from getting too seriously injured.

During a bout, it is the referee's job to enforce the rules to keep the boxers as safe as possible. The referee must also make sure that the boxers are fit to continue boxing during the bout.

A boxer who commits a foul is warned by the referee and may lose points. Too many fouls may result in a boxer being disqualified. Fouls are such actions as hitting below the belt, on the back of the head or neck, or on the kidneys.

FAST TRACK

Other fouls include –

- Butting with the head
- Ducking below waist level
- Hitting an opponent who is down or falling
- Hitting an opponent's eye with the thumb of the glove
- Hitting with the forearm or the inside of the glove
- Kicking
- Remaining in a **clinch** unnecessarily
- Rope holding
- Tripping
- Using elbows in the fight
- Wrestling

Knockouts

A boxer will win the bout if their opponent is knocked out. There are two kinds of knockouts in boxing. One is simply called a *knockout*, or KO. The other is called a *technical knockout,* or TKO.

When a boxer knocks their opponent down, the referee begins counting to ten. The fighter is considered down for the count. If the fallen boxer does not get up before the count reaches ten, then they are counted out. They lose the fight. It is a KO.

A TKO takes place if the referee decides that a boxer is not physically able to keep fighting. The ringside doctor will be called into the ring to inspect the boxer. Only the referee or the fighter's assistants can call for a TKO. In some countries, if a boxer is knocked down three times in one round, his opponent wins the bout on a TKO.

When the boxer's assistants end the match, a towel is sometimes thrown into the ring. This is where the phrase "throwing in the towel" comes from.

A referee signals the end of a fight. This boxer has been unable to stand up and continue with the bout.

Scoring

If the boxing bout is not won on a knockout, then the scores must be added to decide the winner of the bout.

There are two ways of scoring in a boxing match, either the round or the point system.

In the round system, after each round, the judges and referee decide individually which boxer won that round. At the end of the fight, each person votes for the fighter they awarded the most rounds.

In the point system, the referee and judges award each fighter a number of points based on their performance. The boxer scored as the winner by at least two of the officials wins the match.

Boxing Skills

Boxers develop their own style, but they all use the same techniques of offense and defense. These are essential boxing skills.

Good boxers keep in top physical condition, and spend many hours working on their boxing skills by sparring. Sparring is when a boxer trains with another person in the ring.

Amateur and Professional Boxers

There are two types of boxers. There are amateur boxers and professional boxers. Boxers begin as amateurs. Then, if they are successful, they go on to become professional boxers.

Amateurs compete as members of a school or club team. Amateurs do not receive money for boxing.

The world championships for amateur boxing are held every two years. Amateur bouts are also held at the Olympic Games. Many amateurs become professional boxers after competing at the Olympic Games.

An amateur boxer must wear a headguard in a bout.

INFORMATION REPORT - 21

FAST TRACK

Professional boxers fight for money. A professional boxer can make a lot of money, especially as a world heavyweight champion.

Professional boxers usually have both a manager and a trainer. The manager handles **finances**. The manager also organizes the right opponents for their boxer to fight. The trainer works with the boxer to improve their boxing skills.

> Many people want the rules changed to protect the boxers even more.

Weight Groups

The weight of a boxer determines what group they will be boxing in. To fight at a certain level, a boxer may not weigh more than the maximum for that group. For example, a boxer who weighs 110 pounds (50 kg) fights in the flyweight boxing group. The boxer competes against other flyweight boxers. The boxer cannot fight against bantamweight boxers.

Contestants must weigh in on the day of a contest. This is to make sure they are in the competition weight range.

Boxing is still considered a dangerous sport. Many people want the rules changed to protect the boxers even more. Some people think that professionals should wear headguards for boxing contests. They think that professional matches should only have ten rounds. They think that boxers should only punch their opponent's body, not their head.

Is the sport still too dangerous? Should the rules be changed? What do you think?

Amateur and Professional World Boxing Council (WBC) Weights

Weight Groups	Amateur and Olympic	Professional
strawweight (mini flyweight)		up to 105 pounds (47.7 kg)
light flyweight (junior flyweight)	up to 105 pounds (47.6 kg)	up to 108 pounds (49 kg)
flyweight	up to 112.4 pounds (50.8 kg)	up to 112 pounds (50.8 kg)
super flyweight (junior bantamweight)		up to 115 pounds (52.2 kg)
bantamweight	up to 119.1 pounds (54 kg)	up to 118 pounds (53.6 kg)
super bantamweight (junior featherweight)		up to 122 pounds (55.4 kg)
featherweight	up to 125 pounds (56.7 kg)	up to 126 pounds (57.2 kg)
super featherweight		up to 130 pounds (59 kg)
lightweight	up to 132 pounds (59.9 kg)	up to 135 pounds (61.2 kg)
super lightweight (junior welterweight)		up to 140 pounds (63.6 kg)
light welterweight	up to 139 pounds (63 kg)	
welterweight	up to 147 pounds (66.7 kg)	up to 147 pounds (66.7 kg)
super welterweight (junior middleweight)		up to 154 pounds (69.9 kg)
light middleweight	up to 156 pounds (70.7 kg)	
middleweight	up to 165 pounds (74.8 kg)	up to 160 pounds (72.6 kg)
super middleweight		up to 168 pounds (76.2 kg)
light heavyweight	up to 178 pounds (80.7 kg)	up to 175 pounds (79.5 kg)
cruiserweight (junior heavyweight)		up to 190 pounds (86.2 kg)
heavyweight	up to 200 pounds (90.9 kg)	over 190 pounds (86.2 kg)
super heavyweight	over 201 pounds (91.1 kg)	

CHART - 23

THE DEAL

Written by Cam Gregory • Illustrated by Marjorie Scott

> The sun was still thinking about bathing the street in its early-morning glow when Jackson set out on his way to the bakery where he worked before school. He'd been up most of the night listening to his little radio, but it had been worth it. "The Monsoon" had come through for him in the tenth round. The commentator had called it the fight of the century.

Jackson loved boxing and had been following the rise of a local hero. And now, Mathis "The Monsoon" Matheson was the new Heavyweight Champion of the World.

As Jackson turned the corner he saw a wallet lying on the street. There was absolutely no one in sight. The only place open around here at this time of the morning, aside from the bakery, was the local gym where some boxers trained.

"May as well start there," Jackson said to himself.

The first thing Jackson noticed as he wandered down the rickety wooden stairs to the gym was the smell, which was a mixture of sweat and liniment. This was not the typical modern gym that you see on television, with shiny chrome and electronic running machines. This gym was all old brown leather, wooden floors, medicine balls, and a long history of hard work. The rhythmic sounds of people hitting punching bags and ropes hitting the floor added to Jackson's excitement.

"If only," he thought.

"What can I do for you?" said a voice deeper than the Grand Canyon and with almost as much gravel.

Jackson turned and held out the wallet to a man as old as the hills.

"I found this on the street," he stuttered, straining to get the words out, as usual.

The old man's eyes softened as he took the wallet and opened it.

"Thompson!" the old man bellowed, holding the wallet above his head. "I want 20 more minutes on the heavy bag before you get this back. What's your name?" he asked, turning back to Jackson. "And what are you doing on the streets at five o'clock in the morning?"

"I'm Jackson Carruthers. Some mornings I work at the bakery," Jackson replied, embarrassed. He found his stutter so frustrating.

"Nice to meet you, Jackson. I'm Lloyd. I see by the look in your eyes that you like this gym," Lloyd said, holding out his hand, which was the size of a thickly padded boxing glove.

Jackson nodded. He shook Lloyd's hand firmly.

FAST TRACK

"Well, Jackson, you are obviously honest," continued Lloyd. "You must work hard if you are up at this time in the morning. How would you like an after-school job instead of having to get up so early? Don't answer now. Talk to your parents and turn up tomorrow after school if they say it's OK. Now get going, boy, or you'll be late for your bakery job."

Lloyd left Jackson standing where he was, and walked over to the boxing ring. Jackson set off to the bakery, deep in thought.

▶▶▶

Jackson knew his mother would never allow him to work at the gym. She said people who hung out at boxing gyms were no good. He could remember her exact words, "Boxing is a sport filled with violence, and the only goal is to knock someone's head off."

Changing her point of view was not going to happen. He would just go back tomorrow and tell Lloyd, "No."

The next day, he went back to the gym.

"Well, Jackson, I guess your parents said OK?" Lloyd said.

Jackson shook his head.

"That's the deal," Lloyd continued. "You need your mother and father's OK even to come into this gym, let alone work here. What did they say when you asked them?"

"I never knew my father, and my mother doesn't like boxing." Jackson spat out the last word with frustration.

"But you want to work here and learn how to box, don't you?" asked Lloyd, seeing the passion in Jackson's eyes as they stared at the ring where two boxers were sparring.

"Well, then," Lloyd said, grabbing a coat off the chair behind him, "we'd better see if we can change your mother's mind about boxing then, hadn't we?"

"You won't be able to," said Jackson.

"I'll bet I will," replied Lloyd with a smile that lit up his whole face. "Never been beaten out of the ring yet. Let's go!"

▶▶▶

Jackson led Lloyd to the diner where his mother worked.

"You know what, Jackson?" Lloyd said as they walked down the busy street. "I used to coach a boxer who had a stutter just like yours when he was a kid. Now he only stutters when he's nervous. I remember the day when he chose his professional boxing name – Mathis 'The Monsoon' Matheson."

"Yes, that's right, Jackson," Lloyd went on. "Mathis Matheson, the Heavyweight Champion of the World, has a stutter just like yours. That makes you both pretty special, doesn't it? Now, which one is your mother? We've got some negotiating to do."

Jackson pointed out his mother.

"Ms. Carruthers, my name is Lloyd Taylor," Lloyd said before Jackson's mother could say a word about her son being with a strange man. "I was wondering if I could have a word with you about your son."

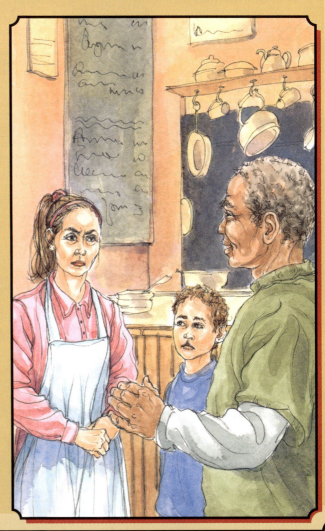

FAST TRACK

They sat down together at a table.

"Well, Ms. Carruthers," Lloyd said, "I'm the owner and manager of the local boxing gym. Jackson came into the gym yesterday morning with a wallet that he'd found on the street."

At the word "boxing," Jackson could see a storm brewing across his mother's face. By the time Lloyd had said that Jackson had been in the gym, the clouds had darkened and there were flashes of thunder and lightning. She crossed her arms. What her face didn't say the rest of her body did.

"Ms. Carruthers, I would like to offer Jackson a job at the gym after school," Lloyd continued.

"Jackson knows my views on boxing and gyms," said Jackson's mother, looking sternly at Jackson. "He also knows that he's got to get his homework finished. I don't want him hanging around gyms after school. He has homework to do."

"Here's the deal," said Lloyd, not put off by what Jackson's mother had said. "Jackson can use my office to do all his homework before he starts cleaning the gym. He can use my computer. I'll make sure he's home by half past eight. If he finishes his work before then, he can use the gym for free."

> At the word "boxing," Jackson could see a storm brewing across his mother's face.

Jackson's mother relaxed a little, but her voice still had a cold wind blowing through it.

"Mr. Taylor, this all sounds great in theory, but what gives you the impression that the people at the gym are any better than the ones hanging out on the streets?"

"Because, Ms. Carruthers," Lloyd replied, "I spent 15 years of my life working behind a desk in the city. During that time, I completed a master's degree in business over the Internet. I had a good job, and I was well rewarded for it, and now I should be relaxing and enjoying my retirement. But no, I brought my wife back here to where I grew up, and it wasn't because I had to, and it wasn't for the money, it was to give something back. That's why you can believe me when I say I run a totally clean gym. If any gym members have any trouble with the police, they're out. If you don't believe me, you can come and have a look, any time."

"If what you've told me is correct, I may need to apologize, but I'll wait until I've seen inside your gym for myself. Then, and only then, will I talk to you about the deal you're offering Jackson," said Jackson's mother.

Jackson couldn't help but smile when he heard this. His mother's answer wasn't a definite yes, but it was a lot closer than he thought Lloyd would get. Lloyd just winked and smiled at Jackson across the table.

> Jackson's mother relaxed a little, but her voice still had a cold wind blowing through it.

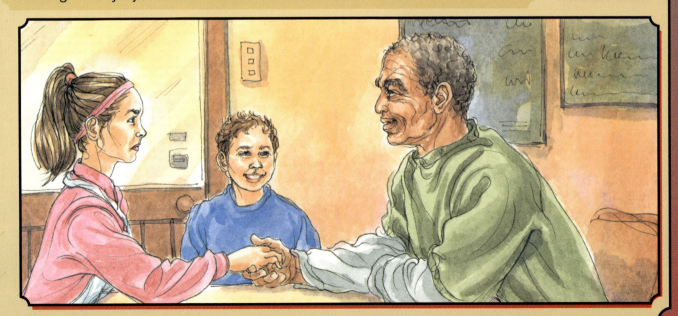

FAST TRACK

BEST NICKNAMES IN BOXING HISTORY

- "Butterbean" – Eric Esche
- "Hands of Stone" – Roberto Duran
- "Iron Mike" – Mike Tyson
- "Bonecrusher" – James Smith
- "Marvelous" – Marvin Hagler
- "Boom Boom" – Ray Mancini
- "Sweet Pea" – Pernell Whitaker
- "The Greatest" – Muhammad Ali
- "The Hitman" – Thomas Hearns
- "The Real Deal" – Evander Holyfield